Mammals

Anita Ganeri

Watts Books
London • New York • Sydney

© 1994 Watts Books

Watts Books
96 Leonard Street
London EC2A 4RH

Franklin Watts Australia
14 Mars Road
Lane Cove
NSW 2066

UK ISBN: 0 7496 1572 9

Dewey Decimal Classification 599

10 9 8 7 6 5 4 3 2 1

Series editor: Pippa Pollard
Editor: Jane Walker
Design: Visual Image
Artwork: Adrian Lascom
Cover artwork: Mainline Design
Photo research: Alison Renwick
Fact checking: Simone K. Lefolii

A CIP catalogue record for this book
is available from the British Library

Printed in Italy by
G. Canale & C. SpA

Contents

What are mammals?   3

How many mammals?   4

Mammals worldwide   6

Shelters and homes   8

Family life   10

Finding food   12

Hunting   14

Moving mammals   16

Self-defence   18

Colours and camouflage   20

Baby mammals   22

Mammal senses   24

Out at night   26

Mammals in danger   28

Things to do   30

Glossary   31

Index   32

What are mammals?

How can you tell if an animal is a **mammal** and not a bird or a fish? There are lots of clues to help you. Mammals have a bony **skeleton** inside their body. They all breathe air through lungs, and they are all **warm-blooded**. All mammals have some fur or hair and most of them have an outer ear. Mammals look after their babies and feed them on milk.

▽ Baby mammals are usually looked after by their mothers.

3

How many mammals?

There are more than 4,500 types of mammal. There are mammals as different in size as whales and shrews, and as different in shape as hedgehogs and giraffes. Mammals can be split into up to 20 separate groups. The **rodent** group is the biggest, with 1,750 members. How many mammals can you think of? Don't forget to count yourself.

▷ Bats are the only mammals that can fly. They have leathery wings.

▽ The blue whale is the biggest mammal and the biggest animal that has ever lived.

Human

4

◁ Long legs and a
long neck make the
giraffe the tallest
mammal.

▽ A pygmy shrew is
about as long as
your thumb. It is the
smallest mammal.

Blue whale

Mammals worldwide

You will find mammals living all over the world. Mammals are warm-blooded animals. This means that the temperature inside their bodies stays the same whatever the weather is like outside. They can survive and keep active even when the weather is very hot or very cold. Many mammals also have other ways of coping with their surroundings.

▽ Jaguars live in the South American rainforest where it is hot and wet. They are superb climbers and swimmers.

▽ Seals hunt for fish underwater. They have flippers for swimming instead of arms and legs.

▷ Camels live in the dry desert. They can survive for weeks without drinking water.

▽ Polar bears have thick coats to keep them warm in the freezing Arctic.

Shelters and homes

Mammals have many different types of home. Some live in underground **burrows**. Others live in hollow trees or in caves. A few even build nests. Some mammals live in their homes all year round. Others only use them as safe places to bring up their babies or to shelter from bad weather.

▷ Bats come out at night to look for food. They spend the day roosting in trees or in caves.

▽ The tiny harvest mouse weaves a ball-shaped nest of grass or corn stalks for its babies.

▽ Gerbils spend the hot desert day in cool underground burrows.

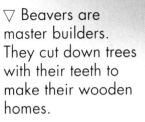

▽ Beavers are
master builders.
They cut down trees
with their teeth to
make their wooden
homes.

Family life

Some mammals live in big family groups. Zebras live in herds, wolves live in packs and dolphins live in schools. The members of the group help to look after each other and to find food. Most groups have a leader. This is usually the biggest, strongest male. In elephant herds, however, the oldest female is in charge.

▽ A group of lions is called a pride.

△ Sloths do not
have large families.
They spend most
of the time on
their own.

▽ Prairie dogs live
in huge groups
called towns.
Sentries guard the
town and sound
the alarm.

△ When ring-tailed
lemurs walk through
the forest, they can
follow the stripy tail
of the lemur in front.

Finding food

Most mammals eat regular meals to keep up their **energy**. Some, such as tigers, are meat-eaters. They have sharp claws and teeth for catching and eating their food. Other mammals, like elephants, are plant-eaters. Their teeth are flat and tough for chewing plants. Many kinds of mammal eat both plants and meat.

▷Giant anteaters use their sharp claws to tear open anthills. Then they lick up the ants with their long tongue.

▽ Elephants use their trunk to pull plants into their mouth.

▽ A sea otter eats crabs. It cracks the shells open on a stone balanced on top of its chest.

△ The Etruscan shrew has a huge appetite for a tiny creature. It may eat three times its own weight in food each day.

Hunting

Some mammals are fierce hunters. They stalk their **prey**, then pounce on it and kill it. Some hunt in teams. They help each other to **track** their prey. Then they work together to catch it. Other mammals hunt alone. Hunting mammals often have very good eyesight and a strong sense of smell. These help them to find and follow their prey.

▷ Grizzly bears scoop up fish in their big, strong paws. They are very successful at fishing.

▽ Wolves hunt in packs. They follow a set pattern of attack. Each wolf knows what it has to do.

▽ Killer whales swim in close to the shore and grab young seals. They sometimes hunt in groups.

Moving mammals

All mammals have to move about to find food, to find a mate and to escape from danger. Some are speedy movers, such as cheetahs and horses. Others, like sloths, move very slowly indeed. Mammals have many ways of moving, depending on where they live. They can run, jump, climb, swim, burrow, swing, fly and glide.

▷ Cheetahs are the fastest runners over short distances.

△ A walrus uses its tusks to help drag itself onto the ice.

▽ Colugos cannot fly but they can glide from tree to tree.

△ Chamois are so sure footed that they can move very quickly, even on the narrowest mountain ledges.

Self-defence

Mammals have different ways of protecting themselves from harm, and of escaping from hungry hunters and other enemies. If there is danger about, fast-moving mammals simply run away. Others bolt underground or disappear up a tree. Some mammals use their horns, teeth, claws, hooves and spines as weapons to defend themselves.

▷ Skunks spray a very smelly liquid at their enemies.

▽ A porcupine has very long quills. These stick into an enemy's skin if it comes too close.

▷ A pangolin's body is covered in scales. The pangolin curls up tightly if there is danger.

▷ If there is danger about, an opossum pretends to be dead.

Colours and camouflage

Some mammals have special patterns of spots, stripes or colours on their coat. Some have a coat which is coloured to blend in with the background. These patterns and colours are called **camouflage**. They help to hide mammals from their enemies. They also help mammal hunters to take their prey by surprise.

▷ No one is sure why zebras are stripy. The stripes may help to hide them in long grass, away from enemies such as hungry lions.

▽ Snowshoe hares are brown in summer. In winter their coat turns white to match the snow.

△ A tiger's stripes help it to hide in the long grass. Tigers can pounce on their prey without being noticed.

Summer

Winter

Baby mammals

All mammals feed their babies on milk and look after them until they can care for themselves. Most mammal babies grow inside their mother and look like their parents when they are born. Others, such as kangaroo babies, are very small and weak when they are born. They have to grow bigger inside their mother's pouch. Two very strange mammals lay eggs. These are duck-billed platypuses and spiny anteaters.

▷ Wildebeest foals can stand and run almost as soon as they are born.

◁ Duck-billed platypuses lay their eggs deep inside riverbank tunnels.

▽ A kangaroo baby, or joey, spends about six months in its mother's pouch. It feeds on milk and grows bigger.

△ A nine-banded armadillo always has four identical babies at a time.

Mammal senses

In general, mammmals have good all-round senses. But a mammal's senses are also suited to its particular lifestyle. For example, a mole cannot see very well but it does not need good eyesight in its underground home. Instead, it has an excellent sense of smell for finding food and making its way around. Cats have sensitive whiskers for feeling their way in the dark.

▷ Hyenas use their excellent senses of hearing and smell to help them hunt.

▽ Some monkeys use bright colours to signal to each other. They need good eyesight to recognise these signals.

△ The fennec fox has huge ears and very good hearing.

Out at night

Some mammals are **nocturnal**. This means that they sleep during the day and look for food at night. It is often safer to be out at night. There are fewer animals about and less competition for food. But nocturnal animals face the problems of finding their way and their food in the dark. To help them, many have special eyesight and stronger senses of hearing and smell than daytime mammals.

▷ Bushbabies have huge eyes for seeing in the dark.

▽ Many bats make very high squeaking sounds. These hit objects and send back echoes. The bats use the echoes to find their way towards food.

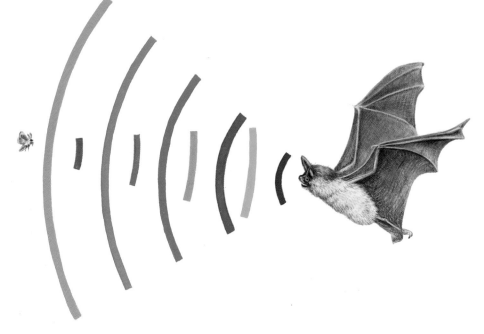

▽ Badgers cannot see
very well but their
hearing is superb.

Mammals in danger

All over the world there are mammals in danger of becoming **extinct**, which means dying out for ever. Some have been hunted for their fur coats and valuable horns or tusks. Others have had their homes destroyed as forests have been cut down, and rivers and seas become **polluted**. Many wildlife groups are trying to save the world's mammals before it is too late.

▷ Giant pandas live in China. They are in danger because from time to time there is not enough bamboo for them to eat.

△ Rhinos are hunted and killed for their horns, even though it is against the law.

△ Golden lion tamarins are very rare. They have lost most of their forest home.

Things to do

If you are interested in mammals and would like to know more about them, there are lots of places you can write to for information. Here are a few useful addresses:

The Mammal Society
Department of Zoology
University of Bristol
BRISTOL
Avon

This society studies British mammals and looks at ways of saving their homes.

World Wide Fund for Nature (WWF)
Panda House
Weyside Park
GODALMING
Surrey
GU7 1XR

The WWF is trying to save endangered animals, including mammals, all over the world.

Watch
c/o The Royal Society for Nature Conservation (RSNC)
22 The Green
Nettleham
LINCOLN
LN2 2NR

A conservation group especially for young people.

Friends of the Earth
26–28 Underwood Street
LONDON
N1 7JQ

This organisation is trying to protect the environment, and the animals living in it.

Glossary

burrow A hole in the ground where a mammal sleeps, hides or raises its babies.

camouflage Special patterns or colours on a mammal's skin or fur. They help the mammal to hide from its enemies or to creep up on its prey by surprise.

energy This gives mammals the ability to move about to find food, shelter or a mate. Mammals get their energy from the food they eat.

extinct No longer exists on the Earth. Mammals which are extinct have all died out.

mammal An animal with a bony skeleton and hair or fur. It breathes air and feeds its babies on milk.

nocturnal This describes any mammal which comes out at night to look for food. Nocturnal mammals sleep during the day.

polluted Made dirty or harmed by waste materials such as chemicals or car fumes.

pouch A type of pocket on the front of mammals like kangaroos and bandicoots.

prey Animals which are hunted as food by other animals.

rodent A mammal such as a mouse, a rat or a squirrel.

skeleton The framework of bones inside a mammal's body.

track To follow.

warm-blooded Able to keep warm without relying on the weather. Warm-blooded animals can stay warm and active even if the weather is cold.

Index

anteater 13, 22
armadillo 23

badger 27
bat 5, 9, 26
beaver 9
burrow 8, 16, 31
bushbaby 27

camel 7
camouflage 20–21, 31
chamois 17
cheetah 16, 17
colugo 17

duck-billed platypus 22

elephant 10, 12

fennec fox 24

gerbil 8
giant panda 29
giraffe 4, 5
golden lion tamarin 29
grizzly bear 15

hare 20
harvest mouse 8
hunting 14–15
hyena 25

jaguar 6

kangaroo 22, 23

lemur 11
lion 10, 21

monkey 24

opossum 19

pangolin 19
polar bear 7
porcupine 18
prairie dog 11

rhinoceros 28

seal 6, 14
sea otter 13
shrew 4, 5, 13
skunk 19
sloth 11

tiger 12, 20

walrus 16
whale 4, 14
wildebeest 23
wolf 10, 14

zebra 10, 21

Photographic credits:
Bruce Coleman (J & D Bartlett) 10,
(W Lankinen) 9, (K Tanaka) 29,
(G Ziesler) 17;
NHPA (B & C Alexander) 7,
(A Bannister) 27, (D Heuclin) 19,
(P Johnson) 25,
(S Krasemann) 13, 23,
(G Lacz) 3, (P Pickford) 21,
(A Rouse) 15.